Piano · Vocal

THE LORD OF THE RINGS

THE MOTION PICTURE TRILOGY

MUSIC BY HOWARD SHORE

Alfred

Produced by
Alfred Music Publishing Co., Inc.
P.O. Box 10003
Van Nuys, CA 91410-0003
alfred.com

Printed in USA.

ISBN-10: 0-7390-5803-7
ISBN-13: 978-0-7390-5803-9

THE PROPHECY

Text by J.R.R. TOLKIEN
Adapted by PHILIPPA BOYENS

Music by
HOWARD SHORE

8

Moderately slow (♩ = 60)

Text based on the poem,
The Prophecy by J.R.R. Tolkien,
adapted by Philippa Boyens

Over the land lies the Shadow
Westward it reaches
On Wings of Darkness

The Tower trembles
To the Tomb of Kings
Doom approaches

Out of the Black Years
Come the words
The Herald of Death

Listen - it speaks to
Those who were not
Born to die:

One Ring to rule them all
One Ring to find them
One Ring to bring them all
And in the Darkness bind them

CONCERNING HOBBITS

Music by
HOWARD SHORE

Moderately (♩ = 104)

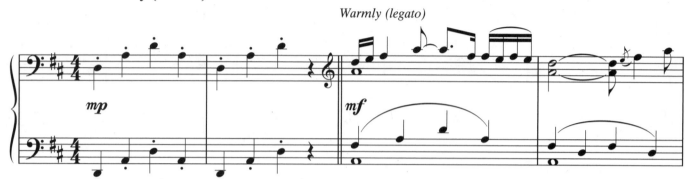

Concerning Hobbits - 4 - 1
32034

Warmly (legato)

THE BLACK RIDER

Music by
HOWARD SHORE

Slowly (♩ = 60)

PROLOGUE

The Black Rider - 5 - 1
32034

Mysteriously, with intensity (♩ = 160)

THE BLACK RIDER

MANY MEETINGS

Music by
HOWARD SHORE

Slowly, flowing (♩ = 80)

(with pedal)

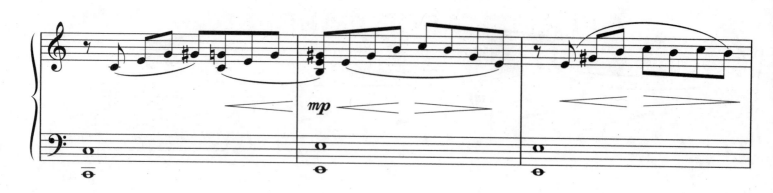

22

LAMENT FOR GANDALF

(featured in "Lothlorien")
performed by Elizabeth Fraser

Text by
PHILIPPA BOYENS

Music by
HOWARD SHORE

Slowly (♩ = 58)

Lament for Gandalf - 3 - 1
32034

Text based on the poem,
Lament for Gandalf
by Philippa Boyens

Solo Text English Translation:

Olorin who once was…
Sent by the Lords of the West
To guard the lands of the East,
Wisest of all Maiar,
What drove you to leave
That which you loved?

No more will you wander
The green fields of this earth
Your journey has ended in darkness.

The bonds are sundered,
The spirit is broken,
The flame of Arnor has left this World.

A great light has gone out.

Chorus Text English Translation:

Our love for this land
Is deeper than the deeps
Of the sea.
Our regret is undying.
Yet we will cast all away
Rather than submit.
What should be shall be.

IN DREAMS

(featured in "The Breaking Of The Fellowship")
performed by Edward Ross

Words and Music by
FRAN WALSH and
HOWARD SHORE

Slowly and freely

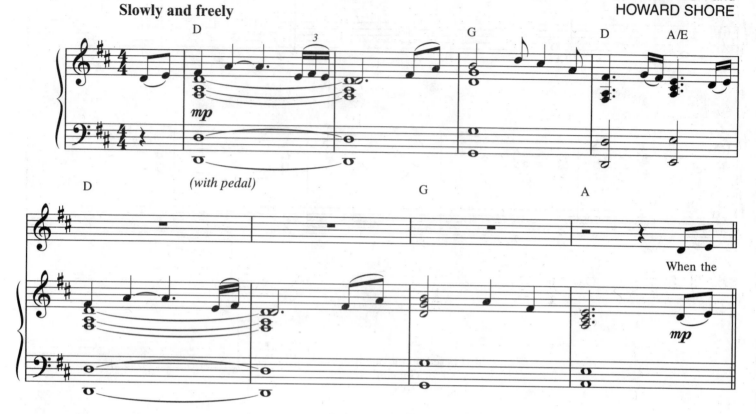

Moderately slow, flowing ♩ = 76

cold of win - ter comes, star - less night will cov - er day.___ In the veil - ing of the sun we will

In Dreams - 3 - 1
32034

MAY IT BE

performed by Enya

Lyrics by
ROMA RYAN

Music by ENYA
and NICKY RYAN

Slowly and freely ♩ = 76

Verse:

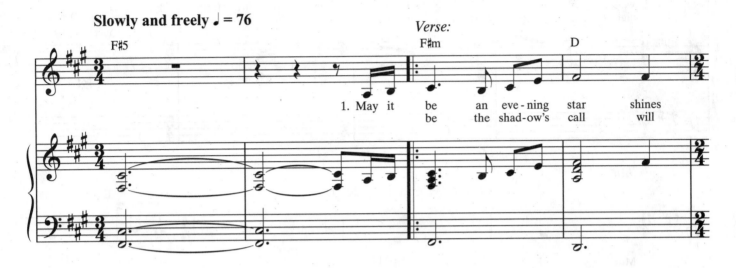

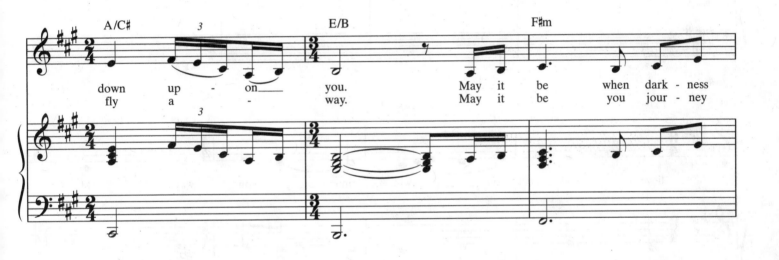

May It Be - 3 - 1
32034

prom - ise lives_____ with - in you

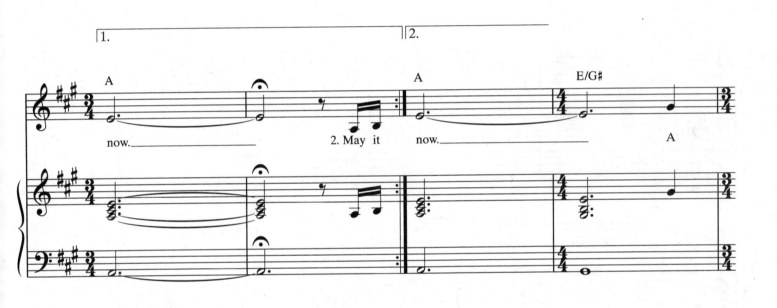

1. now._____ **2.** 2. May it now._____

prom - ise lives with - in you now.

ROHAN

Music by
HOWARD SHORE

Slower ♩ = 63
THE KING OF THE GOLDEN HALL

EVENSTAR

featuring Isabel Bayrakdarian

Text by
J.R.R. TOLKIEN

Music by
HOWARD SHORE

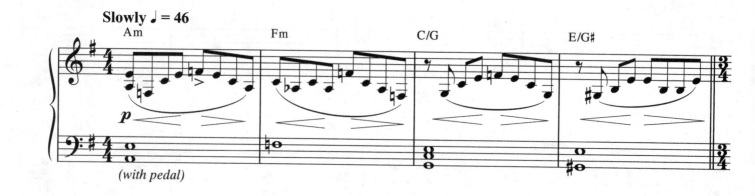

Evenstar - 3 - 1
32034

35

Evenstar - 3 - 2
32034

BREATH OF LIFE

featuring Sheila Chandra

Words by
FRAN WALSH

Music by
HOWARD SHORE

Moderately slow ♩ = 69

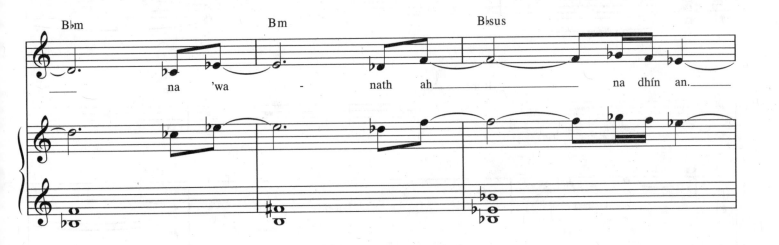

Breath of Life - 4 - 1
32034

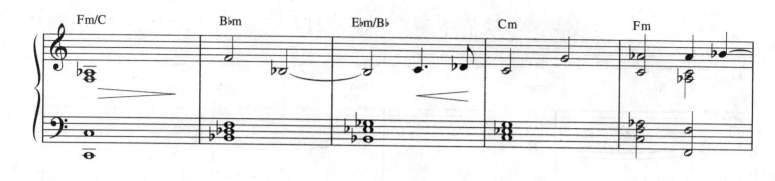

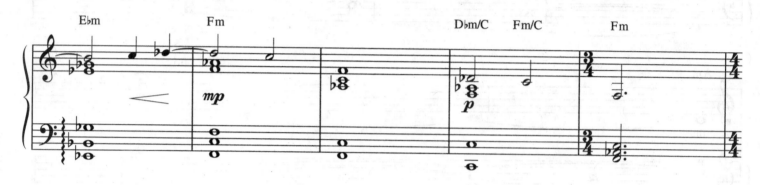

English Translation:

You are not bound to loss and to silence.
For you are not bound to the circles of this world.
All things must pass away,
All life is doomed to fade…
Sorrowing you must go, and yet you are not without hope.

FORTH EORLINGAS

featuring Ben Del Maestro

Text from "The Mearas" by
PHILIPPA BOYENS

Music by
HOWARD SHORE

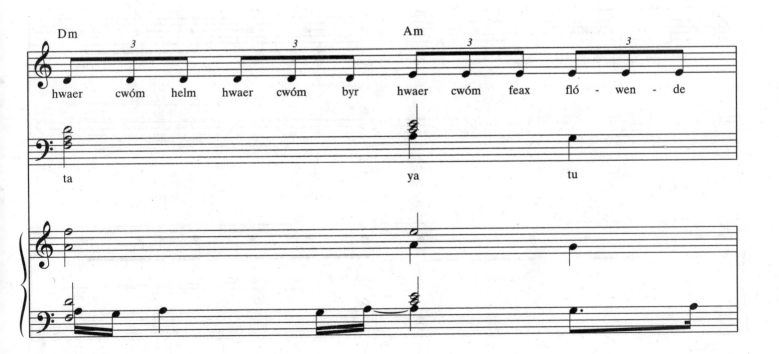

42

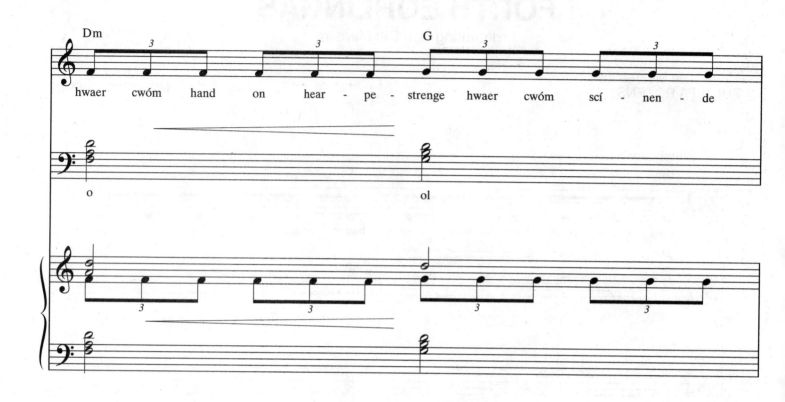

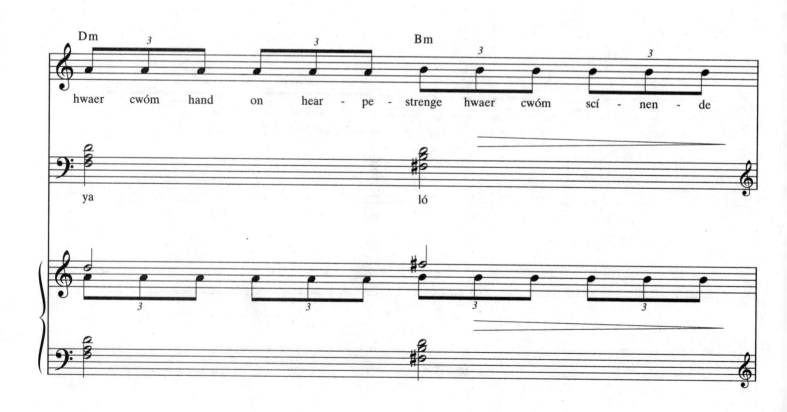

44

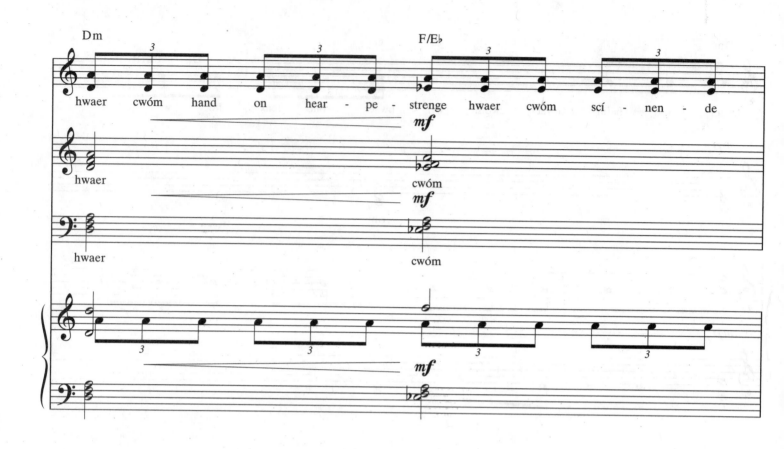

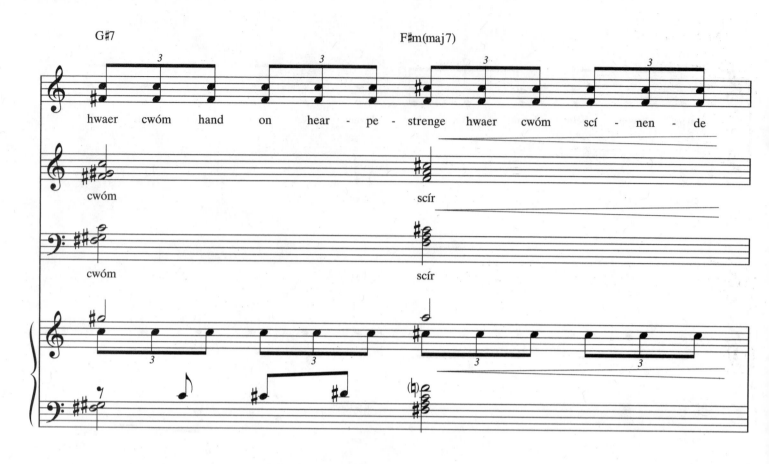

48

(Text from *The Mearas* by Philippa Boyens)

Slower ♩ = 46

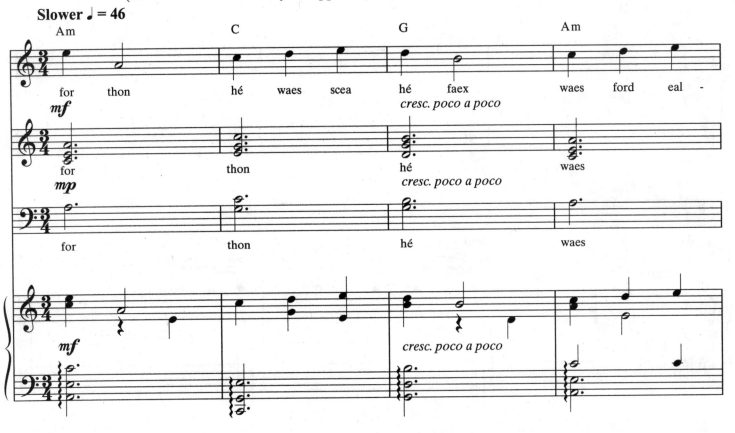

Text based on the poem
The Mearas by Philippa Boyens

In the distance they saw him,
White sun caught in his mane.
Long they called him—
But he would not come.
For he was Shadowfax—
Lord of all Horses.
And he answered to only one.

ISENGARD UNLEASHED

featuring Elizabeth Fraser and Ben Del Maestro

Text from "The Ents" by
PHILIPPA BOYENS

Music by
HOWARD SHORE

Slowly ♩ = 58

HALDIR'S LAMENT performed by Elizabeth Fraser

A little faster ♩ = 160

Performed by Ben Del Maestro

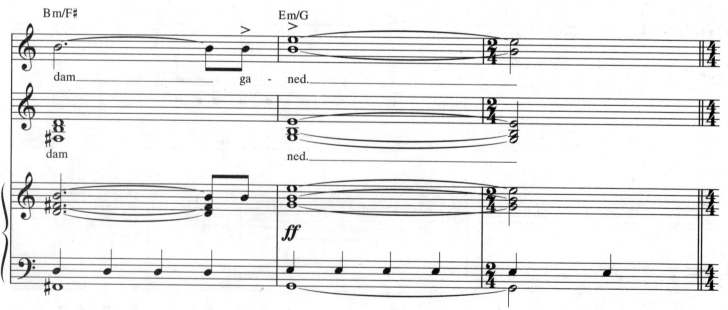

56

Text based on the poem
The Ents by Philippa Boyens

Earth shakes,
Stone breaks
The forest is at your door
The dark sleep is broken
The woods have awoken
The trees have gone to war
Roots rend, wood bends
The Ents have answered the call
Through branches now the wind sings
Feel the power of living things
The trees have gone to war

GOLLUM'S SONG

performed by Emiliana Torrini

Words by
FRAN WALSH

Music by
HOWARD SHORE

Where once was light, now dark - ness falls.

Gollum's Song - 5 - 1
32034

No loy - al friend was ev - er there for me.

Now we say good - bye.

We say, you did - n't try.

These tears you cry have come too late.

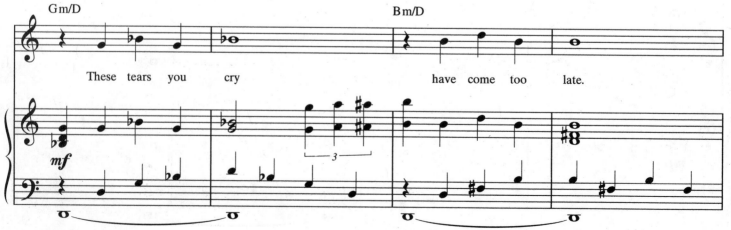

MINAS TIRITH

featuring Ben Del Maestro

Lyrics by
PHILIPPA BOYENS

Music by
HOWARD SHORE

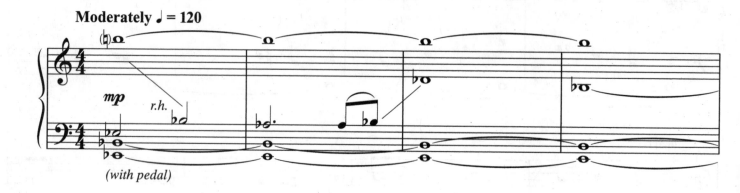

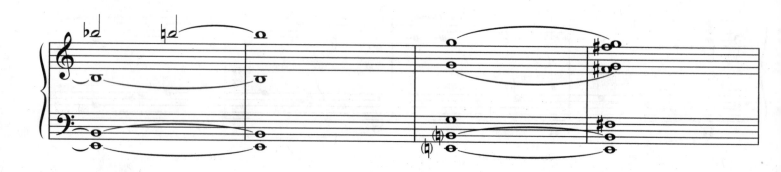

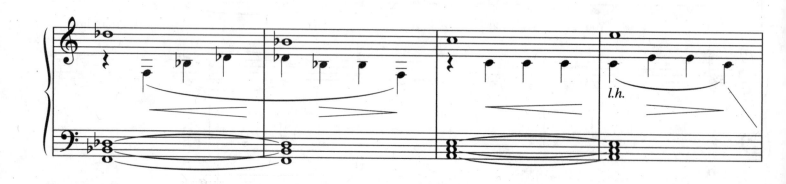

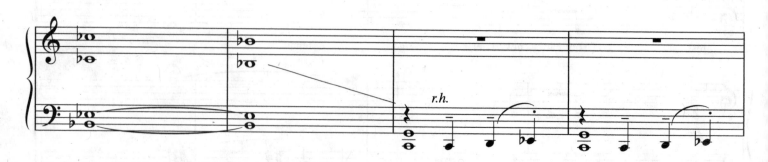

Minas Tirith - 7 - 1
32034

66

MINAS TIRITH SONG

Choir: O - red Gwan - wen ost

in gi - li - ath

simile

Brightly ♩ = 168

MITHRANDIR SONG performed by Ben Del Maestro

Solo boy: Sí - lant ca - lad_____ Dûn_____

_____ Tol-len Ro - chon Lân_____

Men - nen no - red dîn

March ♩ = 148
GONDOR THEME

Text based on the poems
The Retreat from Osgiliath and *The White Rider*
by PHILIPPA BOYENS

THE RETREAT FROM OSGILIATH
Black wings against a pale morning
There is no more light, not in this sun
Call the retreat
There will be no warning
The citadel of the stars is gone
Osgiliath is fallen.

THE WHITE RIDER
Their race was over;
All courage gone.
A light shone in the west –
The White Rider had come.

THE STEWARD OF GONDOR

featuring Billy Boyd

Contains the composition "The Edge Of Night"
Melody by BILLY BOYD
Lyrics by J.R.R. TOLKIEN
Adapted by PHILIPPA BOYENS

Music by
HOWARD SHORE

Slowly ♩ = 50

THE STEWARD OF GONDOR SONG

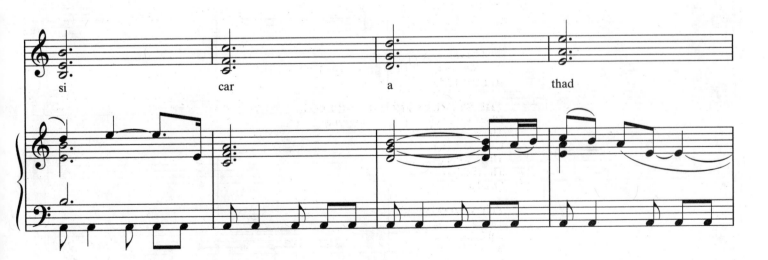

The Steward of Gondor - 5 - 1
32034

A little faster ♩ = 60

73

THE EDGE OF NIGHT performed by Billy Boyd

shade.　　　　　All　shall　fade.　　　All_____

_____ shall_____　　　　　　　fade._____

Text by J.R.R. TOLKIEN,
adapted by PHILIPPA BOYENS

THE LAST SON
You must understand.
He does the duty of two sons now.
For himself; and for the One
Who will not return.

TWILIGHT AND SHADOW

featuring Renée Fleming

Lyrics by
PHILIPPA BOYENS

Music by
HOWARD SHORE

THE GRACE OF UNDÓMIEL SONG *performed by Renée Fleming*

Slower ♩ = 80

An_____ i lu na cu_____ An i

na_____

An_____

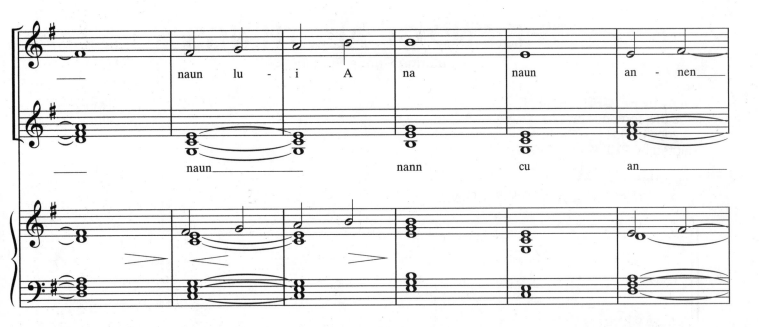

Text from the poem *The Evening Star*
by PHILIPPA BOYENS

THE EVENING STAR
I saw a star rise high in the
Evening sky,
It hung like a jewel,
Softly shining.

I saw a star fade in the
Evening sky,
The dark was too deep and so light died,
Softly pining.

For what might have been,
For what never was.
For a life, long lived
For a love half given.

THE END OF ALL THINGS

featuring Renée Fleming

Lyrics by PHILIPPA BOYENS
Contains the composition "The Eagles"
Lyrics by J.R.R. TOLKIEN
Adapted by PHILIPPA BOYENS

Music by
HOWARD SHORE

Slowly ♩ = 63
THE END OF ALL THINGS SONG

The End of All Things - 9 - 1
32034

Performed by Renée Fleming

THE EAGLES SONG *performed by Renée Fleming*

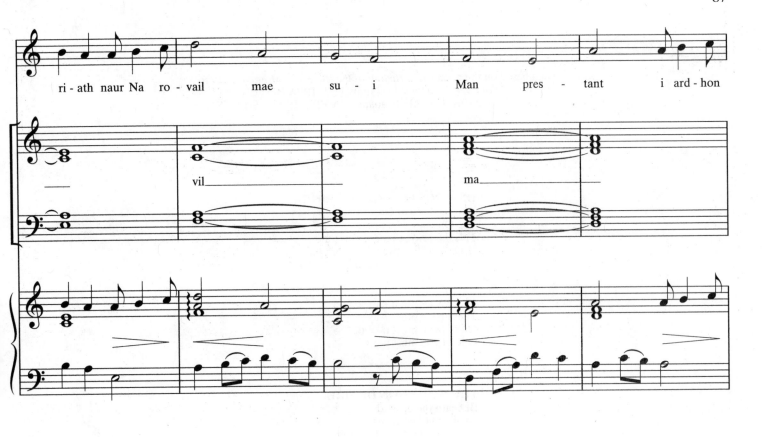

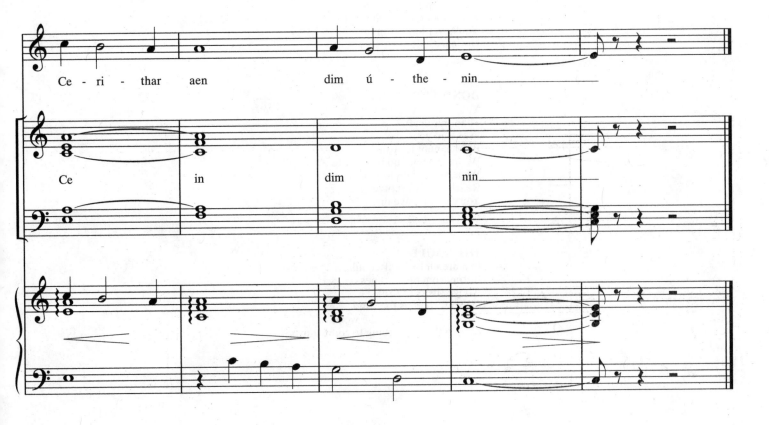

Text based on the poems *Destruction of the Ring*, *The Mountain of Fire*, *Not Once, Not Ever* and *Don't Let Go* by PHILIPPA BOYENS and The Eagles by J.R.R. TOLKIEN, adapted by PHILIPPA BOYENS

DESTRUCTION OF THE RING
Into the fires of Orodruin
The One must be cast;
This the price, that must be paid,
Only thus its power will be undone,
Only thus, a great evil, unmade.

There is no other choice.
There is no other way.
One of you must take it,
One of you must pay.

THE MOUNTAIN OF FIRE
Beneath the ground
Swollen hot with anger
Orodruin releases all its ruin.
Earth rips asunder
Black rain falls.
Here at the end;
The end of all things.
The air is aflame,
All the world is on fire!

NOT ONCE, NOT EVER
You have fallen.
And I cannot reach you.
Every step I willed you on,
Every moment I lead you to this.
You never left my mind,
Not once, not ever.

DON'T LET GO
You want nothing more
Than this death.
I see it in your eye.
But I cannot let you
We have come too far
We have held on too long.
Reach! You cannot let go,
You cannot leave me.

THE EAGLES
In a dream I was lifted up.
Borne from the darkness
Above rivers of fire.
On wings soft as the wind.
What's happened to the world?
Is everything sad going to come untrue?

THE RETURN OF THE KING

featuring Sir James Galway, Viggo Mortensen and Renée Fleming

Contains the composition "Aragorn's Coronation"
Melody by VIGGO MORTENSEN
Lyrics by J.R.R. TOLKIEN

Music by
HOWARD SHORE

Slowly ♩ = 60

THE FRAGRANCE OF ITHILIEN performed by Sir James Galway

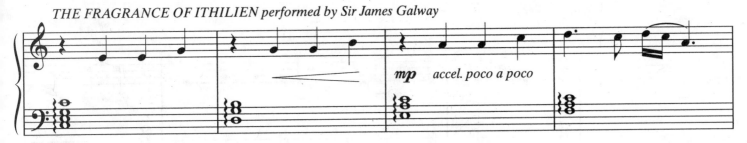

Faster ♩ = 88

Tempo I ♩ = 60

The Return of the King - 10 - 1
32034

90

ARAGORN'S CORONATION *performed by Viggo Mortensen*

Solo: Et Eär-el - lo En-do-ren - na u-tú-li-en

Si - no-me ma-ru-van ar Hil di

Choir: En Si

nyar   tenn'   Am - bar - me_____ ta._____

ny_____   Am_____   ta._____   Hmm.

QUEEN ARWEN SONG performed by Renée Fleming

Slightly faster ♩ = 72

Solo: Ti_____   nú_____   vi_____   el_____

Choir: Hmm

Hmm

A TOAST IN THE SHIRE
performed by Dermot Crehan

Faster ♩ = 112

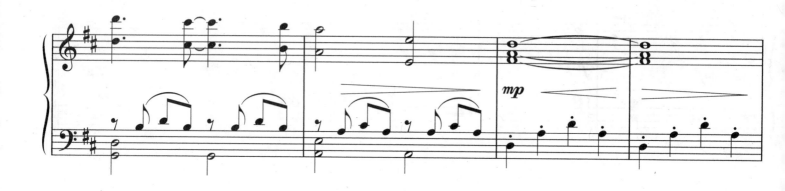

ARAGORN'S CORONATION
Out of the Great Sea to Middle-Earth I am come.
In this place will I abide, and my heirs, unto the ending of the world.

ARWEN - (first appearance)
Tinuviel the elven fair
Immortal maiden elven wise
About him cast her shadowy hair
And arms like silver glimmering

INTO THE WEST

performed by Annie Lennox

Words and Music by
HOWARD SHORE, FRAN WALSH
and ANNIE LENNOX

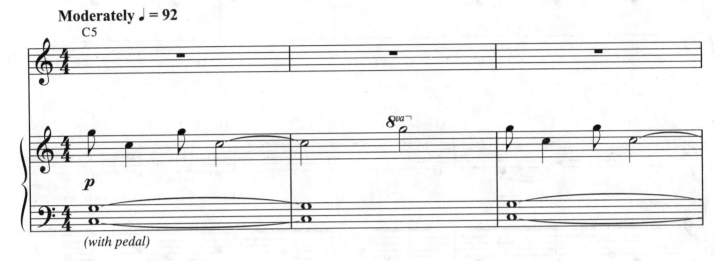

Verse 1:

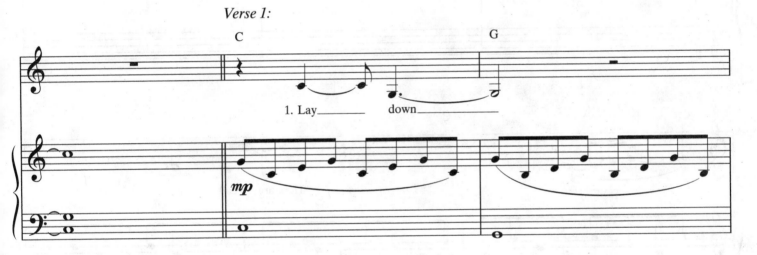

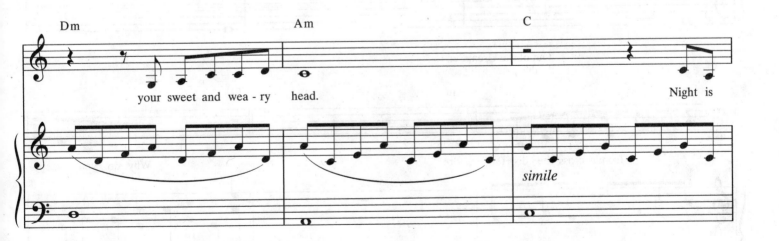

Into the West - 9 - 1
32034

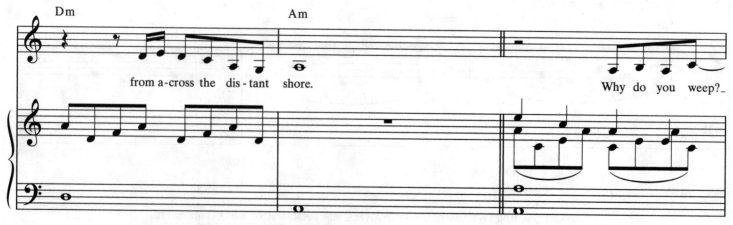